LISTENING CONTOURS

a course in controlled listening
for students of English

Michael A. Rost

LINGUAL HOUSE

Published by
Longman Asia ELT
A division of Longman Asia Ltd
18th Floor, cornwall House
Taikoo Place
979 King's Road
Hong Kong
Fax: (852) 2856 9578

Longman Japan KK
1-13-19 Sekiguchi
Bunkyo - Ku
Tokyo 112
Japan
Fax : (81) 3 3266 0326

and Associated Companies throughout the world

*This book was developed for Longman Asia ELT by Lateral Communications Ltd.
Lingual Houe is an imprint of Longman Asia ELT*

First published 1981
Reprinted 1995 (twice)

Produced by Longman Asia Limited
Printed in China
PPC/08

ISBN 0 940 26410 2

ACKNOWLEDGEMENTS

For this second edition I would again like to express my appreciation to the EFL staff of Athénée Français in Tokyo, particularly to Larry Cisar, Javier Macuaga, Dick Hilbourn, and Tom Matsuda—for offering ideas and testing the lessons.

I would also like to thank the many reviewers of the first edition who contributed ideas and guidance for the revision—especially Ellen Kisslinger, Ken Stratton, Yasuhiro Murayama, and Professor Tomioka. Special appreciation to Keiko Kimura for helping to organize the final manuscript.

Thanks to Oxford University Press for permission to adapt material for two of the talks (T8 and T16) in this series. Those talks are adapted from *Advanced Stories for Reproduction* by L.A. Hill, © Oxford University Press, 1968. Reprinted by permission of Oxford University Press.

The
publisher's
policy is to use
**paper manufactured
from sustainable forests**

CONTENTS

INTRODUCTION

Listening Contours is a series of 30 listening practice lessons designed for high beginning and low intermediate students. Each lesson is based on an extended listening passage, recorded on tape. Pre-listening and post-listening activities are included in each lesson. The central aim of the text is to introduce students to extended listening in English and to make this introduction a successful one.

Description of the Course Materials

Listening Contours consists of these elements:

—a set of 3 tapes containing the pre-listening exercises for each lesson, the 30 lesson talks, follow-up comprehension questions
—a workbook to be used in conjunction with the tapes
—a complete text which contains exercise answers and tape scripts

Format of the Workbook and Tapes

The workbook is divided into 30 units corresponding to the sequence on the tapes. Each workbook unit consists of these sections:

- Pre-listening Vocabulary
  A list of 5 to 7 vocabulary items that appear in the lesson talk. Brief definitions are given on tape.
- Sentence Cues
  A preview of three sentence patterns that appear in the talk. The sentences are recorded on tape and given as a cloze dictation in the workbook.
- Listening Strategy
  A short introduction of the talk and "tips" on what to listen for. This section is recorded on tape.
- the "Talk"
  A monolog given by one of several speakers. Each talk is 2 to 4 minutes long. Talks are controlled for vocabulary, structure, content variation, redundancy, and rhetorical style. Talks are of three main types: Narrative, Process, Classification.
- Comprehension Questions
  Five questions about the talk, recorded on tape.
- After You Listen
  One of several types of written exercises that help the listener to reconstruct important information from the talk.
- Making An Outline
  Instructions for outlining the talk and a partially completed outline frame which reproduces the rhetorical structure of the lecture.
- Application
  Two activities — one calling on the student to summarize the talk using his outline, the other asking the student to construct an outline and give a short presentation on a similar topic.

WORKBOOK SECTION

SPORTS

■ VOCABULARY PREVIEW

The following words and expressions will appear in the talk. Listen and write a short definition for each item.

individual — *done by one person or one thing*

separate — *a part, not together*

compete/competition — *take part in the contest, to try to be better than the other*

perform — *to do, to act*

require — *to be necessary, to need*

■ SENTENCE CUES

Look at the following sentence patterns. Then listen to each sentence.

a.   There are __*two*__ kinds of __*sport*__ .

b.   Besides __*team sport*__ , there is __*another kind*__ .

c.   The main difference is that __*team sport require the separate team*__.

■ LISTENING STRATEGY

> This talk is about two different kinds of sports. As you listen, try to answer these questions: What are the two kinds of sports? What is the purpose of each kind? What are some examples of each kind?
>
> Listen for these classification terms: *there are two kinds, such sports as, besides team sports.*
>
> Now, listen to the talk.

Use this space (or additional paper) for your notes about the talk.

team sport , Individual

base ball   exercise
basket ball   Swimming
Volay ball   sking
*   runing*

2

☐ COMPREHENSION QUESTIONS

Listen to the questions and write your answers on the lines below.

1. What are the two kind of sport

2. What is another name for team sport

3. In foot ball if team A get 7 point and team B get 3 point
   which team win

4. It's possible to keep the score in In dividual sport

5. Swimming is an example of which kind of sport

AFTER YOU LISTEN

Fill in the paragraph below with the ideas from the tape.

There are two main _____ of sports: _____

and _____ . An example of a team sport

is _____ , and an example of an individual

sport is _____ . The purpose of team sports

is _____ . The purpose of individual

sports is _____ . Team sports require

_____ . Individual sports require _____

_____ .

MAKING AN OUTLINE

Organize your notes into an outline. Use the outline frame below. Notice that I and II refer to the MAIN TOPICS. A, B, C, D refer to IDEAS ABOUT THE TOPIC.

SPORTS

I. Team sports

    A.   The purpose is to _____

    B.   They require two _____

    C.   Some examples are _____

II. Individual sports

    A.   The purpose is to _____

    B.   They require only _____

    C.   Some examples are _____

    D.   It is possible to _____

APPLICATION

1. Use your outline to give a short presentation on "sports." Your presentation can be spoken or written. Be sure to cover the main points on your outline.

2. This talk divided "sports" into two categories: team and individual. Think of two other categories for "sports" (e.g. sports that use a ball and sports that don't use a ball/contact sports and non-contact sports). Make an outline similar to the one above. Then give a short presentation on your topic — spoken or written.

MAKING OMELETTES

■ VOCABULARY PREVIEW

The following words and expressions will appear in the talk. Listen and write a short definition for each item.

crack— *to break a hard object*

ingredients— *these items needed to make stirry*

melt— *to become liquid by heating*

frying pan— *kitchen usetensil use for cooking*

chopsticks— *two short pieces of wood use for cooking and eating*

■ SENTENCE CUES

Look at the following sentence patterns. Then listen to each sentence.

a. *First,* __*crack these eggs*__ .

b. *After a couple minutes,* __*turn them over*__ .

c. *When it's* __*cook*__ , __*take it out of the pan*__ .

■ LISTENING STRATEGY

This talk is about how to make omelettes. As you listen, take note of each separate step. Also take note of the ingredients and equipment that are needed to make an omelette.
Listen for these expressions of time order: *first, second, third, after a couple minutes, when both sides are cooked.*
Now, listen to the talk.

Use this space (or additional paper) for your notes about the talk.

cracke the egg into bowl / put

2 - 3 egg

mix the eggs well with the chopsticks untill the mixture has the same color yellow + add st cheese, onion

- melt the butter in the pan

- pour the eggs in hot pan then put the other things on top. then the side cook, turn it over

☐ COMPREHENSION QUESTIONS

Listen to the questions and write your answers on the lines below.

1. *what are omelete make from*

2. *What do you use to mix the eggs*

3. *How many eggs do you use*

4. *Do you put the eggs in the pan before or after you put other ingredients*

5. *Why do you put butter in the frying pan*

AFTER YOU LISTEN

1) Make a list of the ingredients and equipment you need to make an omelette:

eggs   *frying pan*

butter   *bowl*

Cheese , onion   *chopsticks*

2) Put these steps in order:

4 a.   Put some butter into the frying pan.
7 b.   Turn the eggs over.
1 c.   Crack the eggs and put them into a bowl.
8 d.   Remove the omelette from the pan.
3 e.   Cut the ham, cheese, and vegetables into pieces.
2 f.   Mix the eggs.
5 g.   Pour the eggs into the frying pan.
6 h.   Put the cheese, ham, and vegetables on top of the eggs.

MAKING AN OUTLINE

Organize your notes into an outline. Use the outline frame below. Notice that I and II refer to the TWO MAIN STAGES in making an omelette. A, B, C, D, E point to the SPECIFIC STEPS in each stage.

MAKING OMELETTES

I. Prepare the ingredients

    A.   Crack_____ and put _____

    B.   Mix _____ until _____

    C.   Cut _____

II. Cook

    A.   Melt _____

    B.   Pour_____

    C.   Put _____

    D.   Wait_____ turn_____

    E.   _____ from the pan.

APPLICATION

1. Use your outline to explain how to make an omelette. Your explanation can be spoken or written.

2. This lesson's talk explained how to prepare a simple food dish. Think of another simple dish that requires "Preparing" and "Cooking" (e.g. hamburgers, grilled cheese sandwich) or think of a beverage (e.g. coffee, tea, hot cocoa). Make a list of the steps. Use your outline to give a short presentation.

A ROCK IN THE ROAD

■ VOCABULARY PREVIEW

The following words and expressions will appear in the talk. Listen and write a short definition for each item.

destroy— *to break it completely, to make it useless*

earthquake— *violent shaking of the ground*

sphere— *a solid round object*

dig— *to make a hole in the ground*

bury— *to put it in the hole and put it to cover it (dust)*

incline— *a float or floating surface*

■ SENTENCE CUES

Look at the following sentence patterns. Then listen to each sentence.

a. *They decided that* ___*they should try to move it*___ .

b. *I think I can* ___*help you do it*___ .

c. *No matter how* ___*hard they try*___ , *they couldn't* ___*move it*___ .

■ LISTENING STRATEGY

This talk is a short story about what happened in a small village after an earthquake. In this story there is a problem. The problem was solved by a young boy. Listen for a statement of the problem. Then listen for how the problem was solved.

Listen for these time indicators: *a hundred years ago, one day, when it stopped, all of this time, the next morning, last night.*

Now, listen to the talk.

Use this space (or additional paper) for your notes about the talk.

□ COMPREHENSION QUESTIONS

Listen to the questions and write your answers on the lines below.

1. _What road down from the mountain_
2. _Where did the rock stop_
3. _Why did the people laught at the boy_
4. _When was the rock move_
5. _How did the boy move the rock_

AFTER YOU LISTEN

Make a simple drawing that illustrates the story of "The Rock in the Road." Your sketch should include the following items: a *mountain*, *a rock*, *a village*, a *road*, *some people*, *a young boy*, *a rope*, *a shovel*, *and a hole*. The first picture is partly completed.

MAKING AN OUTLINE

Organize your notes about this story into an outline. You can use the outline frame below. Notice that you can divide this story into TWO PARTS. One part is the PROBLEM. The other part is the SOLUTION. The letters A, B, C, D give KEY FACTS and KEY STEPS that explain the problem and its solution.

A ROCK IN THE ROAD

I. Problem

   A.   A large rock _____

          _____ .

   B.   No one could _____

          _____ .

   C.   No one listened to _____

          _____ .

II. Solution

   A.   _____ dug _____

   B.   _____ an incline up to the rock.

   C.   _____ by itself _____ .

   D.   _____ covered _____ with dirt.

APPLICATION

1. Use your finished outline to retell the story of "The Rock in the Road." Follow your outline as you tell the story.

2. This story was a folktale from Japan. Do you know any other folktales or stories? Think of one story you have heard or read. Make a brief outline of the story. Then tell your story.

DOING PUSH-UPS

■ VOCABULARY PREVIEW

The following words and expressions will appear in the talk. Listen and write a short definition for each item.

chest— *the up part of the body*

keep together— *hold two thing next to each other*

palms of the hands— *the front part of the hand*

support— *to hold or hold up*

straighten— *to make straight, to up into line*

■ SENTENCE CUES

Look at the following sentence patterns. Then listen to each sentence.

a.   *As you* ___*lie on the floor*___, *put* ___*your hand next to your shoulder*___

b.   ___*Your hand*___ *should be* ___*next to your shoulder*___.

c.   *In order to* ___*rise yourself*___, ___*straighten your arm*___

■ LISTENING STRATEGY

In this talk the speaker will describe how to do a certain kind of exercise. As the speaker describes the exercise, try to imagine what the exercise looks like. Make a list of the steps.

Listen for verb directions like these: *keep them together, keep it straight, don't lower, stop lowering yourself.*

Now, listen to the talk.

Use this space (or additional paper) for your notes about the talk.

☐ COMPREHENSION QUESTIONS

Listen to the questions and write your answers on the lines below.

1. The push-up excercise is good for what muscle: Chest
arms
2. What part of your body support your wrist during the exercise
3. Should you lie face down or face up: down
4. When you lower your self should your chest touch the floor No
5. Normaly how many push-up should you do in one time
10

AFTER YOU LISTEN

Look at each picture. In each picture the person is doing *something wrong* according-ing to the directions in this talk. Fill in each blank below the picture.

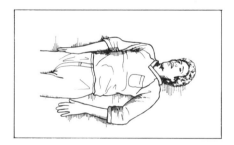

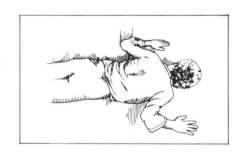

a. He's lying face-up.
He should be _____
_____.

b. His hands are _____
_____.
They should be _____
_____.

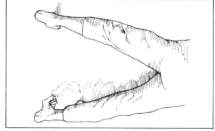

c. His feet are _____.
They should be_____.

d. His body touched the floor.
He should have stopped lowering him-self when _____
_____.

MAKING AN OUTLINE

Make an outline of "Doing Push-Ups." It is possible to divide this talk into two parts: Beginning Position and Movement. These MAIN PARTS are shown by I and II. The letters A, B, C indicate the STEPS.

DOING PUSH-UPS

I. Beginning position

    A.   Lie on the floor, face down.

    B.   _____ legs _____.

    C.   _____ hands _____.

II. Movement

    A.   _____ away from the floor.

    B.   _____ until you almost touch the floor.

    C.   _____ several times.

APPLICATION

1. Use your finished outline to explain how to do push-ups. Be sure to follow the steps on your outline. When you explain, you can add information.

2. This lesson's talk was about an exercise. Think of another exercise that you know how to do (e.g. sit-ups, yoga exercises, warm-up exercises before running). Make a short outline of the important steps. Then explain the purpose of the exercise and how to do it.

THE ANCIENT
CHINESE CALENDAR

■ VOCABULARY PREVIEW

The following words and expressions will appear in the talk. Listen and write a short definition for each item.

The miracle not real n look like

dragon— *very large snake*

rooster— *a male chicken*

cycle— *oven fit it soft*

keep track of— *keep a record of*

chart— *paper or list of important information*

consult— *to go to a person or a book in order to get an advice.*

■ SENTENCE CUES

Look at the following sentence patterns. Then listen to each sentence.

a. *You can* ___figure out the animal of every year___ .

b. *In ancient times,* ___It have Some Surmise law___ .

c. *It's used to* ___keep track of months and years___ .

■ LISTENING STRATEGY

This talk will describe the cycle of the old Chinese calendar. As you listen, make a list of the animals in the cycle and note a year for each animal. Also note how the calendar was used in the past.

Listen for these transitional markers: *therefore, similarly, one area of, another area of, on the other hand.*

Now, listen to the talk.

Use this space (or additional paper) for your notes about the talk.

Choose married partner
1949, 1961, Rat 1984 dragon dog
ox 1985, 1973 note — choose Job (profession)
tiger hamster → sheep boar
rabit monkey
rooster

14

☐ COMPREHENSION QUESTIONS

Listen to the questions and write your answers on the lines below.

1. _According to the Chinese Calender what's animal for teis year?_ Rat

2. _What's animal came after the dragon? Snake_

3. _How often the cycle repeat itself? 12 years_

4. _What two area of life the calender use for?_

5. _the Chinese calendar till have a lot of meaning for people?_

AFTER YOU LISTEN

Below is a list of the animals in the Chinese calendar. After the name of each animal, write the date of the most recent year for that animal.

boar 12 _____   rabbit 1 _____

dog 11 _____   rat _____

dragon 5 _____   rooster 10 _____

horse 7 _____   sheep _____

monkey 9 _____   snake _____

ox 2 _____   tiger 3 _____

MAKING AN OUTLINE

Make an outline of this talk about the "Chinese Calendar." Notice that the talk has two parts. The FIRST PART of the talk described the animals in the cycle. The SECOND PART talked about USES OF THE CALENDAR. Your outline would also divide the talk in this way. The first part of the talk is simply a LIST. The second part of the talk contains some IDEAS.

THE ANCIENT
CHINESE CALENDAR

I. The Chinese calendar was divided into 12 year cycles.

   A.   Each year had the name of an animal.

      1. rat   7. horse

      2. _____   8. _____

      3. _____   9. _____

      4. rabbit   10. rooster

      5. dragon _____   11. _____

      6. _____   12. _____

   B.   Each animal repeated every _____ .

II. The calendar had some uses.

   A.   The calendar was used for selecting _____ .

   B.   The calendar was used _____ .

APPLICATION

1.   Use your outline to explain what the Chinese calendar is and what uses it had. Your explanation can be spoken or written.

2.   One use of the Chinese calendar was as a system to tell a person's future. That means it was a system of "fortune-telling." Are you familiar with any other systems of "fortune-telling"? (e.g. the signs of the zodiac, palm-reading, Tarot cards). Find out about a system of fortune-telling. Make a brief outline of the system. Then explain it briefly.

LIFTING THINGS

■ VOCABULARY PREVIEW

The following words and expressions will appear in the talk. Listen and write a short definition for each item.

squat— to lower your self by bending your knee

support— to hole up

spread— to extend , to move a part

waist— midle of your body , the part of your body above the hips

hips— the bone the form of half circle at the top of your leg

■ SENTENCE CUES

Look at the following sentence patterns. Then listen to each sentence.

a. Try to __get__ as _____squat_____ as possible.

b. __lift__ with __your leg__ , not with __back__ .

c. It's easy to __hurt your back__ when you __lift st heavy__ .

■ LISTENING STRATEGY

This talk will describe the correct way to lift heavy objects from the floor. As you listen, try to imagine what the correct position and movement look like.
Listen for these condition markers: *If you _____, when you _____.*
Now, listen to the talk.

Use this space (or additional paper) for your notes about the talk.

back traight
-tand up slowly
- lift witth your leg , not your back

17

☐ COMPREHENSION QUESTIONS

Listen to the questions and write your answers on the lines below.

1. What is squat mean?

2. When you lifting should you keep your knees together?
   NO

3. Why you should keep your back straight?
   because if your bend lower your back will be hurt

4. Where should you put your hand? under the object

5. Which muscle actualy lift the object? leg

AFTER YOU LISTEN

1) Fill in the blanks.

Many people ___hurt___ their backs when they ___try___

to ___lift___ heavy things from the ___floor___ . It's

___easy___ to hurt your ___back___ when you try to pick

up ___something heavy___ . However, if you ___lift___

heavy objects ___right___ , you probably won't hurt

your back.

2) Describe the correct way to lift heavy objects. Use these verbs: squat, keep...straight, get close, spread, put (hands), stand up.

_____

_____

_____

_____

MAKING AN OUTLINE

Notice that the talk is simply a SERIES OF STEPS. Since the series is rather short, it is not necessary to divide it into stages.

LIFTING THINGS

I. _____ close to the object.

II. _____ straight.

III. _____ knees.

IV. _____ under the object.

V. _____ slowly

APPLICATION

1. Use your outline to explain the correct action for lifting heavy objects from the floor.

2. This lesson's talk explained how to perform an action. Think of some other actions (e.g. washing dishes, shaving, cleaning a room). Make a list of all the specific actions. Then use your list to give an explanation of the action.

OPENING LOCKS

■ VOCABULARY PREVIEW

The following words and expressions will appear in the talk. Listen and write a short definition for each item.

cylinder—

pin—

combination—

dial—

disc—

■ SENTENCE CUES

Look at the following sentence patterns. Then listen to each sentence.

a.   *This kind of* _____ *is called* _____ .

b.   *When you* _____ , _____ .

c.   *Inside* _____ , *there are* _____ :

■ LISTENING STRATEGY

This talk gives a description of two kinds of locks. The speaker will briefly explain how each lock works. As you listen, pay attention to these words that indicate direction and location: *inside the lock, into the lock, inside the cylinder, under each pin, lift up out of the cylinder, the front of the lock, to the left, to the right, in a line.*
   Now, listen to the talk.

Use this space (or additional paper) for your notes about the talk.

□ COMPREHENSION QUESTIONS

Listen to the questions and write your answers on the lines below.

1. _____

2. _____

3. _____

4. _____

5. _____

AFTER YOU LISTEN

Label the parts of the illustrations.

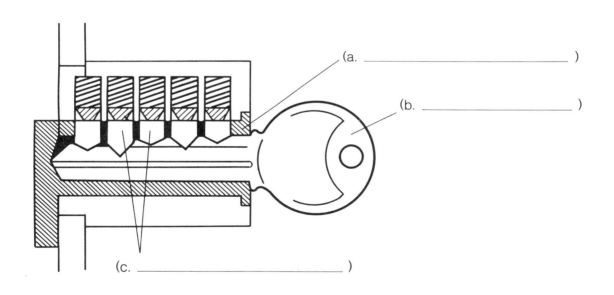

(a. _____)

(b. _____)

(c. _____)

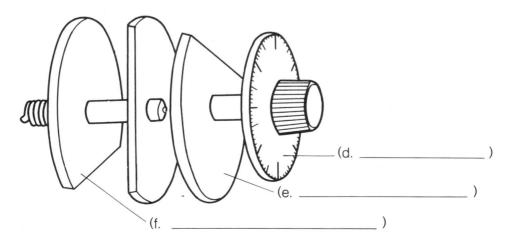

(d. _____)

(e. _____)

(f. _____)

21

MAKING AN OUTLINE

Make a brief outline of this talk. Use the outline frame below. You will have two MAIN HEADINGS (I, II). A and B will give the main facts for each heading.

OPENING LOCKS

I. Opening a cylinder lock

   A.   Put _____ into _____ .

      1. There are five _____ .

      2. The key has to _____ exactly under _____

      _____ .

   B.   Turn _____ .

      1. The pins _____ .

      2. The lock is _____ .

II. Opening a combination lock

   A.   Turn the _____ on the front of the _____ .

      1. The _____ has several _____ on it.

      2. The _____ turns the _____ inside the _____ .

   B.   Select the correct _____ of turns.

      1. Turn the dial to the _____ then to the _____ , then to the

      _____ to the correct numbers.

      2. If _____ ,

      the lock will open.

APPLICATION

1. Use your outline to explain what a cylinder lock and combination lock are. Don't actually read your outline. Only refer to it as a reminder when you are speaking or writing.

2. This lesson's talk described how some simple devices work. Think of some other devices (e.g. toaster, record player, typewriter, water faucet). Find out how they work (by consulting an encyclopedia). Then make a short outline of the information.

TWO WHITE MICE

■ **VOCABULARY PREVIEW**

The following words and expressions will appear in the talk. Listen and write a short definition for each item.

wire—

pipe—

pet store—

confused-

squeeze—

■ **SENTENCE CUES**

Look at the following sentence patterns. Then listen to each sentence.

a. *He told him that he was going to* _____ .

b. *When he heard* _____ , *he ran* _____ .

c. _____ *at one end* _____ ; _____ *at the other end.*

■ **LISTENING STRATEGY**

This story will describe a problem that two electricians had when they were working in a house. Listen for a description of the problem. Then listen for how the problem was solved.

In this talk there is some direct speech and some indirect speech. Listen for these indirect speech phrases: *Harry asked Frank how... Frank told him that...* When you hear the words "I" and "you", you are listening to direct speech, as in these phrases: *"I think I know how..." "I'll show you..." "What are you doing?"*

Now, listen to the talk.

Use this space (or additional paper) for your notes about the talk.

☐ COMPREHENSION QUESTIONS

Listen to the questions and write your answers on the lines below.

1. _____

2. _____

3. _____

4. _____

5. _____

AFTER YOU LISTEN

Draw a rough sketch of the story in four pictures. Include these items in the sketch: *pipe, wire, two mice, two men.* The pictures should also show these actions: *tie, squeeze, run, untie.*

MAKING AN OUTLINE

Make a brief outline of this story. Notice that we can divide this story into "Problem" and "Solution." These would be the GENERAL HEADINGS of the outline (I, II). The capital letters (A, B, C, D) give the MAIN IDEAS of the story. Notice that these ideas (A, B, C, D) are SUMMARY IDEAS. To write summary ideas, you have to use your own words to explain. Naturally, there are several ways to give summary ideas.

TWO WHITE MICE

I. Problem

    A.   The electricians had to _____

    _____ .

    B.   _____ , _____ .

II. Solution

    A.   One electrician (Frank) bought _____

    _____ .

    B.   Frank tied _____

    _____ .

    C.   Frank held the _____

    _____ .

    D.   The other electrician (Harry) held _____

    _____ the other _____ .

    E.   Harry _____

    _____ .

    F.   The male mouse _____ .

    G.   _____ came out the opposite end _____

    _____ .

    H.   The wire was _____ .

APPLICATION

1.   Use your finished outline to retell the story of "Two White Mice."

2.   This story had a "problem" and a "solution." The solution was rather unusual. Can you think of a problem that might have an unusual solution (e.g. how to get a cat down from a tree, how to get rid of cockroaches from an apartment, how to cross a wide river). Think up an unusual solution to the problem, one that *might* work. Make a brief outline of the problem and the solution. Then tell your story.

DICTIONARIES

■ VOCABULARY PREVIEW

The following words and expressions will appear in the talk. Listen and write a short definition for each item.

alphabetical order— *in oder accordiy to the alphabet; a b c orkr* *letter of*

phonetic alphabet— *a system of symbol to shuw pronunciation*

look up— *to find st. in the list*

approximately— *close to, about, nearly*

■ SENTENCE CUES

Look at the following sentence patterns. Then listen to each sentence.

a. The first thing that ___*dictionnaries will tell you*___ is ___*the spelling*___ .

b. There are ___*3*___ things that ___*are important*___ .

c. It will tell you how ___*a word pronunciation*___ .

■ LISTENING STRATEGY

This talk will briefly explain three types of information that you can find in a dictionary. Listen for a statement of each type of information.
Listen for these introductory phrases: *the first thing is, the second thing is, the third thing is.*
Now, listen to the talk.

Use this space (or additional paper) for your notes about the talk.

1) *Spelly*

2) *pronunciation : Sound alphabet*

3) *meaniy of word*

☐ COMPREHENSION QUESTIONS

Listen to the questions and write your answers on the lines below.

1. _In what order are the words listed? A, B c_

2. _How the pronunciation of the word showing?_

3. _How can you find out a work usage?_

4. _In the dictionaries will the word think come before the word thin?_

5. _Which the phonetic alphabet is common for you in the international Alphabet dictionary_

AFTER YOU LISTEN

1) Fill in the blanks in the following paragraph.

In a dictionary words are _____ in _____

order. The _____ of the words is given in

a phonetic alphabet. If you _____ a word, you can

_____ its meaning.

2) Circle the set of words which is in alphabetical order.

a. power	b. poor	c. poverty
poverty	poverty	poor
poor	power	power

MAKING AN OUTLINE

Make an outline of this talk about "Dictionaries." The talk is divided into three topics about dictionaries. Your outline should separate these TOPICS (I, II, III). The capital letters will be MAIN IDEAS about the topics.

DICTIONARIES

I. Spelling

    A.   A dictionary gives the correct _____

        _____ .

    B.   Words are listed in _____

II. Pronunciation

    A.   A dictionary gives _____

        _____ .

    B.   _____ is given by _____

        _____ .

III. _____

    A.   A dictionary explains _____

        _____ .

    B.   Example sentences show _____ .

        _____ .

APPLICATION

1. Use your outline to give a summary of three types of information contained in dictionaries.

2. Look carefully at the dictionary that you use. Make an outline that shows *all* the kinds of information that your dictionary gives you (e.g. spelling, pronunciation, word origin, part of speech, etc.) Use your outline to explain the features of your dictionary. (Note: Instead of a dictionary, you may use another book: a textbook, an atlas, an encyclopedia, etc.)

A TRICK WITH NUMBERS

■ VOCABULARY PREVIEW

The following words and expressions will appear in the talk. Listen and write a short definition for each item.

trick—

house number—

multiply—

add—

subtract—

■ SENTENCE CUES

Look at the following sentence patterns. Then listen to each sentence.

a. *If you _____ , you'll get _____ .*

b. *In other words, _____ .*

c. *After you _____ , _____ .*

■ LISTENING STRATEGY

This talk will describe a simple trick that you can do with numbers. The problem involves simple arithmetic — adding, subtracting, multiplying, and dividing. As you listen, you will have to follow directions. The speaker will tell you to write down certain numbers, to add, subtract, and so on. As you listen, write down the example that the speaker gives.
Listen for these expressions of time order: *first, after you do this, then, the fifth step is.* Now, listen to the talk.

Use this space (or additional paper) for your notes about the talk.

☐ COMPREHENSION QUESTIONS

Listen to the questions and write your answers on the lines below.

1. _____

2. _____

3. _____

4. _____

5. _____

AFTER YOU LISTEN

Identify which steps are wrong. If the directions are wrong, correct them.

a. Write down your house number.

b. Multiply this number by 4.

c. Add 2 to this number.

d. Multiply this number by 15.

e. Add your age to this total.

f. Add the number of days in a year.

g. Multiply this total by 615.

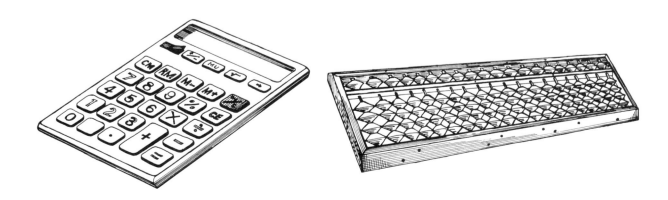

MAKING AN OUTLINE

Make an outline of this "trick." Your outline should first give the STEPS (I). Then your outline should explain the RESULT (II).

A TRICK WITH NUMBERS

I. Steps

    A.   Write down _____ .
        (example: 73)

    B.   _____ .
        (example: 73 × _____ = _____)

    C.   Add _____ .
        (example: 146 + _____ = _____)

    D.   Multiply by _____ .
        (example: _____ = 7550)

    E.   Add _____ .
        (example: _____)

    F.   _____ 365.
        (example: _____)

    G.   _____
        (example: _____)

II. Result

    A.   The first part of the number is _____ . (e.g. 73)

    B.   The second part of the number is _____ . (e.g. 26)

APPLICATION

1. Use your outline to retell this "trick" with numbers. Tell the trick to someone who will follow the steps that you give.

2. This trick was really a simple mathematical process with several steps. Some steps *reversed* other steps. You can also make a simple mathematical trick; the result will be the same number that you begin with (e.g. write down your height, multiply it by 5, subtract your height, add your height plus 100, divide by 5, subtract 20 — this is your original height). Outline a similar mathematical process. Use your outline to tell the process to someone. See if the result is always the same.

VITAMINS

■ VOCABULARY PREVIEW

The following words and expressions will appear in the talk. Listen and write a short definition.

chemical substance— *everything make up of chemical*

natural foods— *food ias) fruit vegetable that grow naturaly*

grains— *a small hard seed or fruit of plants*

nervous system— *nerf site and brain*

virus— *small element they can cause disease*

kidneys— *two body organ they control liquid in the body*

■ SENTENCE CUES

Look at the following sentence patterns. Then listen to each sentence.

a.   If we don't ___*get enough vitamin*___, we'll ___*have health problem*___

b.   ___*This vitamin*___ is necessary for ___*the eyes*___ .

c.   ___*this vitamin*___ is contained in ___*grain*___ , such as ___*wheat or rices*___ .

■ LISTENING STRATEGY

This talk is about the different vitamins that we need. Each vitamin is needed for a different purpose. Take note of the purpose that each vitamin has. Each vitamin also has particular sources in food. Take note about which foods are the best sources of each vitamin.
Listen for each change of topic. When the speaker mentions a new vitamin (A, B, C, etc.), the topic is changing.
Now, listen to the talk.

Use this space (or additional paper) for your notes about the talk.
A — eyes, skin — carrot green vegetable + liver
B — general — soybean bean nut grain → nervous sys. brain
C — muscle healthy virus → all fruit orange, berry, strawberry
D — egg — nut → strong bone, kidney
E — heart blood → almond, walnut, bocoli circulation

☐ COMPREHENSION QUESTIONS

Listen to the questions and write your answers on the lines below.

1. What is Vitamin

2. Which Vitamin can be produce by the body : D

3. What is the best source of Vitamin C : berry : from berry   *orange fruit*

4. Which vitamin is ~~good~~ *important* for blood circulation : E

5. Carrot and liver contain a lot which Vitamin A

AFTER YOU LISTEN

1) Match the vitamins with their main sources.

Vitamin A   beans, nuts, grains

Vitamin B   fruits, especially berries

Vitamin C   nuts, green vegetables

Vitamin D   carrots, green vegetables, liver

Vitamin E   fish, eggs, milk products

2) Which vitamins are needed for which of the parts of the body?

nervous system   _____

blood circulation _____

bones   _____

eyes   _____

kidneys   _____

skin   _____

muscles   _____

MAKING AN OUTLINE

Make an outline of this talk about "Vitamins." The talk is clearly divided into HEADINGS (Vitamin A, Vitamin B, etc.). Under each heading, there are KEY FACTS about why the vitamin is important and its sources. Notice that under "Sources" there are several SPECIFIC EXAMPLES. These specific examples are listed as 1, 2, 3.

VITAMINS

I. Vitamin A

    A.   This vitamin is important for _____

        _____ .

    B.   Sources

        1. fish liver oil

        2. _____

        3. _____

II. Vitamin B

    A.   Vitamin B is important _____ .

    B.   There are several B vitamins.

    C.   Sources

        1. _____

        2. _____

        3. _____

III. Vitamin C

    A.   Vitamin C is important for _____ and for _____

        protection of _____ .

    B.   _____

        1. _____

        2. _____

IV. Vitamin D

    A.   Vitamin D is important for _____

            _____ .

    B.   _____

            1. _____

            2. _____

            3. _____

V. Vitamin E

    A.   _____

            _____ .

    B.   _____

            1. _____

            2. _____

APPLICATION.

1. Use your outline to give a brief presentation about "Vitamins." Your presentation can be a written or spoken summary.

2. This lesson's talk was about a general medical topic. Think of another topic related to medicine or health (e.g. nutrition, protein, vaccines). Use an encyclopedia or other reference materials. Make a brief outline of your information. Then give a short presentation.

THE WORLD'S LARGEST CITIES

■ VOCABULARY PREVIEW

The following words and expressions will appear in the talk. Listen and write a short definition for each item.

determine— *Know clearly, figure out*

define— *, to give a clear meaning*

compare— *to look at difference, between two or more thing*

estimate— *to say appropriate number*

metropolitan area— *area around the city and include the city*

CITY NAMES: Bombay, Buenos Aires, Calcutta, Jakarta, London, Los Angeles, Mexico City, Moscow, New York, Peking, Paris, Seoul, Shanghai, Tianjin, Tokyo.

■ SENTENCE CUES

Look at the following sentence patterns. Then listen to each sentence.

a. *First of all, it isn't easy to* _determine where the city is_ .

b. *Nowadays, nearly all* _city_ *have* _large urban area_ .

c. *When we talk about* _the city_ *, we often mean* _the whole area around it_ .

■ LISTENING STRATEGY

This talk will be about the populations of the world's largest cities. At first the speaker will discuss why it is hard to determine population size. Later, the speaker will give some estimates of city populations.

Listen for these "rewording" expressions: *so when we talk about population.../so we really can't compare because.../so we can say that.../* Also listen for these classifying expressions: *in the first group, in the second group, in the third group.*

Now, listen to the talk.

Use this space (or additional paper) for your notes about the talk.

Population		
1	2	3
Calcutta	los Angeles	paris
New york	London	Bombay
Tokyo	peking	Seoul
	Moscow	

36

☐ COMPREHENSION QUESTIONS

Listen to the questions and write your answers on the lines below.

1. _Why is it dificult to determine the population of the cits_

2. _Why is it dificult to compage the population figure?_

3. _According to the 1991 estimate what are the 3 largest cits in the world?_

4. _Accordiy to the estimate is Paris bigger than Jakarta?_

5. _All these city which one is the largest: Sao Palo Bom Bay, London_

AFTER YOU LISTEN

Rank these cities in terms of population. The largest in this list will be #1, the second largest in this list will be #2, etc.

2 Peking   1 Sao Paulo   3 Seoul

1 Calcutta   2 Moscow   1 Mexico City

1 New York City   1 Shanghai   1 Tokyo

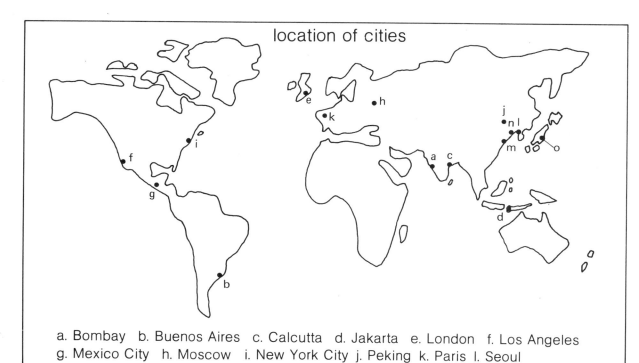

location of cities

a. Bombay b. Buenos Aires c. Calcutta d. Jakarta e. London f. Los Angeles
g. Mexico City h. Moscow i. New York City j. Peking k. Paris l. Seoul
m. Shanghai n. Tianjin o. Tokyo

MAKING AN OUTLINE

Make an outline of this talk on the "World's Largest Cities." The first part of the talk discusses the difficulty in determining the size of a city's population. The first part of your outline should deal with this "Difficulty in Measuring Population Size."

The second part of the talk is actually a list of some of the world's largest cities. In the talk this list of cities is divided into THREE GROUPS. The second part of your outline can also be divided into three groups or HEADINGS.

THE WORLD'S LARGEST CITIES

I. Difficulty in _____

    A.   It's difficult to _____ .

    B.   It's difficult to _____

    _____ .

II. Some of the largest cities

    A.   Major group (1981 estimate)

        1. Tokyo _____   — _____

        2. _____   — 12 million

        3. _____   — _____

        4. _____   — 10 million

        5. _____   — 10 million

        6. Sao Paulo   — _____

    B.   Second group

        1. Los Angeles

        2. _____

        3. _____   all approximately _8.5_ to _10_ million

        4. _____

        5. _____

C. _____

    1. Paris

    2. _____ ⎫

    3. _____ ⎬   _7 — 8.5 million_

    4. _____ ⎭

APPLICATION

1. Use your outline to give a brief presentation about "The World's Largest Cities."

2. Find information about the largest cities in one particular country. Use an encyclopedia or an almanac. Make a list of the cities and their estimated populations. Try to find out population figures for two different years (e.g. for 1970 and for 1980) in order to see how the population is changing. Give a short presentation based on your information.

MEAN AND MEDIAN

■ VOCABULARY PREVIEW

The following words and expressions will appear in the talk. Listen and write a short definition for each item.

statistics—

calculate—

divide—

quantities—

misleading—

eliminate—

■ SENTENCE CUES

Look at the following sentence patterns. Then listen to each sentence.

a. *Any group of _____ has both a _____ and a _____ .*

b. *_____ and _____ are _____ each other.*

c. *It's a more _____ of _____ .*

■ LISTENING STRATEGY

The speaker in this talk will explain two terms, mean and median, that are used in statistics. As you listen, take note of how to find the mean and how to find the median. As you listen, write down the examples that the speaker gives.

Listen for the expressions that indicate examples: *in this case, for example, let's say, in our example, in this sample.*

Now, listen to the talk.

Use this space (or additional paper) for your notes about the talk.

☐ COMPREHENSION QUESTIONS

Listen to the questions and write your answers on the lines below.

1. _____

2. _____

3. _____

4. _____

5. _____

AFTER YOU LISTEN

1) Find the mean for this series of numbers:

   11, 7, 8, 15, 12

2) Find the median for the same series.

3) Match the word on the left with the correct definition on the right.

statistics	a. to get rid of, to take away
calculate	b. to state an approximate number, to guess roughly
eliminate	c. the study of numbers and relationships
misleading	d. not showing a true relationship or fact
accurate	e. to figure out by using numbers
estimate	f. exact, true

MAKING AN OUTLINE

Your outline for this talk might be divided into three parts: TOPIC ONE ("Mean"), TOPIC TWO ("Median") and COMPARISON OF TOPIC ONE AND TOPIC TWO (Comparison of Mean and Median).

For both the mean and median, give the MAIN POINTS: (A) what it is (definition) and (B) how to find it or calculate it.

For your comparison (III), give two main points of comparison.

MEAN AND MEDIAN

I. Mean

    A.   It is the arithmetic average of _____

    B.   How to get the mean.

        1. Add up _____

        2. Divide _____

    C.   Example

        1. Add the quantities: 90, 87, 83, 74, 72, 68, 59 = 533

        2. Divide by _____ : _____ = _____

II. Median

    A.   It is the middle _____

    B.   How to _____

        1. Put the scores _____

        2. Count _____

        3. _____ into equal groups.

        4. The _____ is the median.

    C.   Example

        1. Put in order: 42, 36, 98, 44, 30 = __, __, __, __, __.

        2. _____

        3. _____

        4. _____

III. Comparison

   A.   Mean and median are different ways to _____

         _____ .

   B.   The median is often a more _____ of _____

         _____ .

APPLICATION

1.   Use your outline to give a summary of "Mean and Median." Be sure to include an example when you give your presentation.

2.   This lesson's talk explained two mathematical terms. Think of one other mathematical term (e.g. square root, area, volume). Explain how to calculate the term. Be sure to make complete notes before you begin.

MAKING PEANUT BUTTER

■ VOCABULARY PREVIEW

The following words and expressions will appear in the talk. Listen and write a short definition for each item.

food processing plant— *a place where food packed to be sold*

shell— *a hard covering*

roast— *to cook over hot fire*

tub— *a large pot or bucket*

paste— *thick soft mixture*

■ SENTENCE CUES

Look at the following sentence patterns. Then listen to each sentence.

a.   It's a ___*very easy*___ process with ___*6 basic*___ steps.

b.   After being ___*roast*___ -ed, they have to be ___*crack*___ -ed.

c.   In order to ___*pick the peanut*___ , we have to ___*pull up*___ .

■ LISTENING STRATEGY

This talk will describe the process of making peanut butter. There are six steps. Listen for each step.
Listen for these time markers: *the first step, after the first step is complete, after shelling, after being roasted, next, then.*
Now, listen to the talk.

Use this space (or additional paper) for your notes about the talk.

1) *Picking the peanut*
2) *shell: take off the hard covering [machine]*
3) *Roasted*
4) *Cracked or round off (grind)*
5) *add spice*
6) *put it the jar glass*

☐ COMPREHENSION QUESTIONS

Listen to the questions and write your answers on the lines below.

1. _Where the peanut grow ?   below the ground_
2. _Where the shelling of the peanut done : machine_
3. _How long the peanut has to be roasted : Several minute_
4. _Why the spice added to the peanut butter ? Add flavor_
5. _What kind of container the peanut batter usualy Sold glass jar_

AFTER YOU LISTEN

Make sentences about "Making Peanut Butter" using the words given. You will have to add some additional words.

1. step, peanut butter, picking

   _____

2. peanuts, grow, ground

   _____

3. peanuts, roasted, minutes

   _____

4. grinding, makes, paste

   _____

5. machines, remove, shells, peanuts

   _____

MAKING AN OUTLINE

This talk is a PROCESS. It explains how something is done. According to the talk there are six basic steps. Your outline will then be divided into six parts.

MAKING PEANUT BUTTER

I. _____

   A. The whole peanut plant is _____

   B. The peanuts are _____

II. _____

   A. The shells must be _____

   B. This work is done at _____

III. _____

   A. The peanuts _____ in large ovens.

   B. _____ improves _____

IV. _____

   A. The peanuts are ground by machine.

   B. The peanuts become _____

V. _____

VI. _____

   A. The peanut butter is poured _____

   B. The jars are _____

APPLICATION

1. Use your outline to give a summary of how peanut butter is made. Your summary can be spoken or written.

2. Peanut butter is a kind of "processed food." Think of another processed food (or drink). Some possible topics are: cheese, soft drinks, instant soup. Find out how it is made. Consult an encyclopedia or other reference material. Make an outline that gives all the important steps. Then give a short presentation.

A LIGHT BULB

■ VOCABULARY PREVIEW

The following words and expressions will appear in the talk. Listen and write a short definition for each item.

groove— *a hallow chanel that's cut into a hard Surface*
EX: a record has a hallow groove

conducting wires— *the metal wire that cary electrical current*
cavity

tungsten— *very hard kind of medal*

nitrogen— *a kind of gas , it S._____ N*

argon— *a kind of gas + Symbol is AR*

melt— *to cause to became solf*

■ SENTENCE CUES

Look at the following sentence patterns. Then listen to each sentence.

a.   *If it _____ -s, the bulb won't Work .*

b.   *These are used so that Tungsten doesn't melt.*

c.   *It is the part that actually produces for light.*

■ LISTENING STRATEGY

The speaker in this talk will describe the basic parts of a light bulb. The speaker will also explain the function of each part. There are some special terms that the speaker will use.

Listen for these expressions that indicate function: *it has grooves so that.../it is the part that produces.../it's necessary to.../they are used so that...*

Now, listen to the talk.

Use this space (or additional paper) for your notes about the talk.
electrical source
1) bottom of the light bulb (contact pist) : make contact with
2) the metal base (hold the light bult in the lamp)
3) the conducting wires (2 wires: conduting the electricity into the light bulb
4) tungsten : produces for light (midle of bulb)
5) gas (2 gas : nitrogen + argon): protect the tungsten from smelt
6) glass covering : keep the gas inside the bulb

☐ COMPREHENSION QUESTIONS

Listen to the questions and write your answers on the lines below.

1. What is the purpose of the metal base?

2. What is the conducting wires do?

3. Which part of the light bulb actually produce the light? Stugter

4. Why it necessary to have Nitrogen and argon inside the light bulb

5. What will happen if the glass covering broaken

AFTER YOU LISTEN

Label the parts of the illustration.

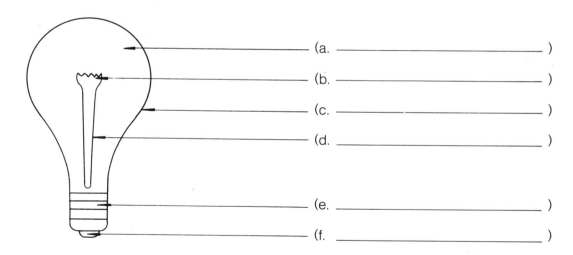

(a. _____)

(b. _____)

(c. _____)

(d. _____)

(e. _____)

(f. _____)

MAKING AN OUTLINE

Notice that in this outline frame, "A" refers to location; "B" refers to function. There are six parts (I-VI).

A LIGHT BULB

I. Contact point

    A. It's at the _____ of the light bulb.

    B. It makes contact with _____ .

II. Metal base

    A. It's at _____ .

    B. It holds _____ .

III. Conducting wires

    A. They are two _____ that go from _____

        to _____ .

    B. These _____ into the bulb.

IV. _____

    A. This is in _____ .

    B. It _____ when it becomes _____ .

V. _____

    A. It is _____ .

    B. It _____ .

VI. _____

    A. _____

    B. _____

APPLICATION

1. Use your outline to explain the functions of the different parts of a light bulb. Your summary can be spoken or written.

2. A light bulb is an electrical device. Think of another electrical device (e.g. a toaster, an electric shaver, a food blender). Find out how it works by consulting an encyclopedia or other reference material. Give a short presentation. You may need to use illustrations.

WILD BOARS

■ VOCABULARY PREVIEW

The following words and expressions will appear in the talk. Listen and write a short definition for each item.

attack— *to attempt to hurt something or some one lots of things, wood to*

trap— *a device for capturing animal used*

weapon— *a device to harm a person or animal.*

conclusion— *a discovery that in make by studying*

Indian corn— *a type of corn that has several color of corn kernal*

materials— *items or equiptment use to make something are*

■ SENTENCE CUES

Look at the following sentence patterns. Then listen to each sentence.

a. *He said that he would* __Solve the problem__ .

b. *He spent* __the first week__ __watch__ -ing __the animal__

c. *Little by little, more and more* __boars went there__ .

■ LISTENING STRATEGY

> This talk is a short story about how a problem was solved. The problem was caused by wild boars and was solved by a hunter. As you listen, take note of how the problem was solved. There are several steps in the solution of this problem.
>
> Listen for these time expressions: *used to be, for many years, finally, the following week, by the end of two months, the entire week, at first, little by little, during this time.*
>
> Now, listen to the talk.

Use this space (or additional paper) for your notes about the talk.

New Zealand - Boars land
attact people
Peter Thomason

— boars like to eat Indian corn

☐ COMPREHENSION QUESTIONS

Listen to the questions and write your answers on the lines below.

1. What did Thomason do during the first week on the Island
   (study the boars) : Watching the boars

2. How did Thomason can get the boar to come to one place
   He feed them Indian Corn

3. Why did Thomason want the boar all to come to one place
   It's easy for him to catch the boars all

4. Why didn't Thomason use the weapon : He don't want to scare
   the boar so that they don't come to one place
   the boars, So they go somewhere

5. What was Thomason reward : 10,000 dollars

AFTER YOU LISTEN

Put these events in chronological (time) order. (1-14).
In this list "he" refers to Thomassen. The order of some of the events is given in parentheses ( ).

1. He built a fence. (11)

2. He came to Boarland. (4)

3. The government sent a letter to Thomassen. (2)

4. He spent 20 hours a day watching the boars. (5)

5. He began to spread some corn in the forest. (7)

6. The boars ate the corn that he spread out. (9)

7. He led the people into the forest. (12)

8. He discovered that the boars liked Indian corn. (6)

9. He accepted the government's offer. (3)

10. The people tried to kill the boars. (1)

11. He received a check from the government. (14)

12. None of the boars would eat the corn that he spread out. (8)

13. He asked for building materials. (10)

14. He said that the boars weren't dangerous anymore. (13)

MAKING AN OUTLINE

There are a lot of individual events in this story. When you make your outline, it will *not* be possible to include every event. When there are a lot of events (or steps), you may have to SUMMARIZE some of the events into one event.

It is possible to divide this story into two parts: Problem and Solution.

WILD BOARS

I. Problem

    A.   Boars used to be a problem in Boarland.

        1. They attacked _____

        2. They _____

    B.   The village people were unable to

        1. They tried to _____

        2. They tried to _____

II. _____

    A.   Thomassen studied _____

    B.   Thomassen discovered that _____

    C.   Thomassen _____ and gradually

        _____

    D.   _____

        _____

APPLICATION

1.   Use your completed outline to retell the story of "Wild Boars." Refer to the outline only when necessary.

2.   Do you know any stories like this one? If not, prepare to tell the story from a movie you have seen or a book you have read. Outline the story first and refer to the outline when you tell the story.

BRITISH AND AMERICAN ENGLISH

■ VOCABULARY PREVIEW

The following words and expressions will appear in the talk. Listen and write a short definition for each item.

idiomatic expression— *a phrase or a sentence who mean it not clear from the word only*

vowel— *in the sound that make without stopping breatheand and without (R l a o u) any friction*

SOME PHONETIC SYMBOLS

/æ/ — the symbol for the vowel sound in "apple"

/a/ — the symbol for the vowel sound in "father"

/ɔ/ — the symbol for the vowel sound in "bought"

/o/ — the symbol for the vowel sound in "boat"

■ SENTENCE CUES

Look at the following sentence patterns. Then listen to each sentence.

a. *One difference between* __British__ *and* __American English__ *is* __vocabulary__

b. *In addition to* __some common words__, *many* __idiomatic expressio__-s *are* __different__ .

c. *Most of the* __sound__ -s *of* __2 dialect__ *are* __the same__

■ LISTENING STRATEGY

In this talk the speaker will go over some basic differences between British English and American English. Take note of the differences. Also take note of any examples that are given.

Listen for these expressions that show differences: *almost exactly the same, minor differences, used in different ways, spelled differently, an American would say… but a Britisher would say…*

Now, listen to the talk.

Use this space (or additional paper) for your notes about the talk.

Vocabulary, pronunciation and spelling I: centre
(1)   (2)   (3) A: center
boot — trunk   vowel, be/ /a/ /ɔ/ /o/
E I can't call you
telepho : E: I brig you up tonight] A: I can not call you | E: colour
idiom. A: I call you up ___   A: color

53

☐ COMPREHENSION QUESTIONS

Listen to the questions and write your answers on the lines below.

1. What is the British English word for the back compartment of the car   boot

2. How do you say this sentence in British English" He call me up last night"
   He bring me up last night

3. Are most of the sound in American English as British English are different
   No, very small #

4. How is the word Center spell in British English?" Centre"

5. I'm American English the word labor is spell "Labor" how do
   you think it will spell in British English "labour"

AFTER YOU LISTEN

Fill in the following table about some differences between British and American English.

	British	American
VOCABULARY	flat (a place to live)	Apartment
	boot	trunk (the back of a car)
	(to telephone)	
SPELLING	centre	Center
	colour	color
	labour	labor
PRONUNCIATION	/ɔ/ or /a/? call	/ɔ/ or /a/? call
	/æ/ or /a/? can't	/æ/ or /a/? can't

54

MAKING AN OUTLINE

This talk contains a few EXAMPLES of differences between British and American English. Examples may be listed as 1, 2 UNDER the FACT for which they are examples. In other words, you have to *identify* your example.

If there is only one example, you can write it directly under the fact as "e.g." (a Latin abbreviation that means "one example from many examples").

BRITISH AND AMERICAN ENGLISH

I. Vocabulary differences

  A Some _____ are different.

     1. _____ (British) vs. _____ (American)

     2. _____ (British) vs. _____ (American)

  B. Many _____ are different.
     (e.g. " _____ " (British) vs. " _____ " (American))

II. _____

  A. /a/ (as in "can't) (British) is sometimes /æ/ (American)

  B. /ɔ/ (as in "call") (British) is sometimes /a/ (American)

III. _____

  A. Words ending in _____ are sometimes spelled

    _____

  B. Words ending in _____

    _____

APPLICATION

1. Give a summary of this lesson's talk. Your summary can be either spoken or written. Refer to your finished outline.

2. British and American English are dialects of one language. All languages have dialects that are spoken in different parts of a country or different parts of the world. Take another language that you know (e.g. Spanish, Arabic, Japanese). What dialects does it have? Where are they spoken? How are they different? Think about these questions. Make your information into an outline. Then give a short presentation.

ANOTHER TRICK
WITH NUMBERS

■ VOCABULARY PREVIEW

The following words and expressions will appear in the talk. Listen and write a short definition for each item.

consist—

omit—

magic—

digit—

result—

■ SENTENCE CUES

Look at the following sentence patterns. Then listen to each sentence.

a. *Multiply the number that _____ by _____ .*

b. *The result of _____ -ing _____ is_____ .*

c. *Even though you _____ , _____ will _____ .*

■ LISTENING STRATEGY

In this talk the speaker will explain a trick that you can do with numbers. As you listen, you will have to follow some directions using basic arithmetic. As you listen, write down the example that the speaker uses. The example will help you to understand the steps.

Listen for expressions that show a result: *the result of, the result will be, if you do this, you'll get...*

Now, listen to the talk.

Use this space (or additional paper) for your notes about the talk.

□ COMPREHENSION QUESTIONS

Listen to the questions and write your answers on the lines below.

1. _____

2. _____

3. _____

4. _____

5. _____

AFTER YOU LISTEN

Choose the correct item for each description.

1. a series of a single figure

   a. 12345

   b. 22222

   c. 13579

2. the "magic number" (in this talk)

   a. 63

   b. 12345679

   c. 77777777

3. the "magic factor" (in this talk)

   a. nine times the number that you chose

   b. a list of the numbers one through nine

   c. a number that consists of a series of sevens

MAKING AN OUTLINE

This "trick" has STEPS (I) and a RESULT (II). Notice that for every step you need an ACTION (verb).

ANOTHER TRICK WITH NUMBERS

I. _____

    A.   Write down _____

    B.   Choose _____

    C.   _____

         _____

    D.   Multiply _____

II. _____

    A.   The result of I.D. is a _____

    B.   Any choice in I.B. will give a result that _____

         _____

APPLICATION

1. Use your outline to retell this "trick" with numbers. Tell the trick to someone who will follow the steps that you give.

2. Here is a mathematical problem (one that involves geometry): The figure below is made up of circles one centimeter in radius. What is the area of the shaded (dark) part? Several steps are needed to solve this problem.
   Can you think of *another* problem that requires several steps to solve? Prepare an outline that gives the necessary steps.

MAKING CHOCOLATE

■ VOCABULARY PREVIEW

The following words and expressions will appear in the talk. Listen and write a short definition for each item.

cocoa—

oval-shaped—

row—

bitter—

crush—

■ SENTENCE CUES

Look at the following sentence patterns. Then listen to each sentence.

a. *It takes about _____ to _____ .*

b. *_____ is a kind of _____ that _____ -s _____ .*

c. *When it's _____ , _____ turns _____ .*

■ LISTENING STRATEGY

This talk will describe the basic process used in making chocolate. Listen for what the cocoa fruit is like. Then listen for the various steps.
Listen for expressions that show a connection of steps: *When...../After.....*
Now, listen to the talk.

Use this space (or additional paper) for your notes about the talk.

☐ COMPREHENSION QUESTIONS

Listen to the questions and write your answers on the lines below.

1. _____

2. _____

3. _____

4. _____

5. _____

AFTER YOU LISTEN

Read each statement. Each statement is false according to the talk that you have heard. Change the sentences in order to make them true.

a. The cocoa fruit is round.

No, it isn't. It's _____ .

b. The cocoa fruit has a thin, soft skin.

No, it doesn't. It has _____ .

c. The trees each have about 40 or 50 cocoa fruits.

No, they don't. They each have _____ .

d. When the fruit is ripe, the outside skin turns light yellow.

_____

e. The raw cocoa beans are rather sweet.

_____

f. It takes about three or four days for the beans to dry.

_____

g. When the beans are dried, then turn dark red.

_____

MAKING AN OUTLINE

This talk is a description of a PROCESS. A process has STEPS. In this case we can divide a group of steps into STAGES. A "stage" is a series of *related* steps: steps that happen in the same location or at approximately the same time.

For this talk, two separate stages might be "getting the cocoa" and "making the chocolate."

Notice that many of the specific facts (e.g. I.A. 1 and 2) *do not* explain *how* the process is done. Some facts give *related information* about the process.

MAKING CHOCOLATE

I. _____

    A.   Picking the cocoa fruit.

        1. The ripe fruit is _____

        2. Each tree has _____

    B.   _____

        1. It must be _____

        2. Each fruit contains _____

    C.   _____

        1. _____ for 3-4 weeks.

        2. _____ brown and small.

II. _____

    A.   Preparing _____

        1. The beans must be _____

        2. _____ mixed with _____

    B.   _____

        1. _____ has to be

        _____

        2. _____ becomes _____

    C.   Cooling

        1. The liquid is cooled.

        2. _____

APPLICATION

1. Use your completed outline to give a summary of "Making Chocolate."

2. This lesson's talk gave the basic steps of making chocolate. The first step was getting the fruit; then some changes were made in the "raw material." Think of another food in which a natural food product is changed before it is sold (e.g. coffee, tea, wine). Find out the basic steps involved in making the final product. Give a short presentation.

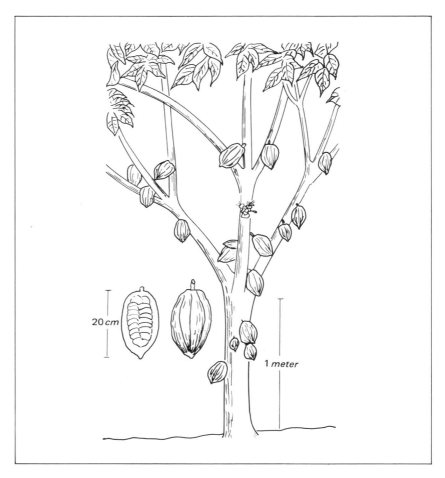

20 cm

1 meter

A cocoa tree

BANANA CAKE

■ VOCABULARY PREVIEW

The following words and expressions will appear in the talk. Listen and write a short definition for each item.

flour—

baking powder—

shortening—

measuring cup—

chop—

■ SENTENCE CUES

Look at the following sentence patterns. Then listen to each sentence.

a. *Before you* _____ *, make sure that* _____ .

b. *Continue* _____ *-ing until* _____ .

c. _____ *should be* _____ *-ed* _____ *before* _____ .

■ LISTENING STRATEGY

In this talk the speaker will give you a recipe for how to make a banana cake. In order to follow the recipe, you will have to take notes of what ingredients are used, what measurements are used, and in what order the ingredients are used.

Listen for words that indicate amounts: 2/3 of a cup, 1 1/4 teaspoons, 1 cup, 2 1/3 cups. Listen for the indication of temperature: *degrees Farenheit or degrees Centigrade.*

Now, listen to the talk.

Use this space (or additional paper) for your notes about the talk.

□ COMPREHENSION QUESTIONS

Listen to the questions and write your answers on the lines below.

1. _____

2. _____

3. _____

4. _____

5. _____

AFTER YOU LISTEN

Write down the ingredients that are needed in this recipe. In the column on the right, write down the amounts of each item that are needed.

bananas	3 or 4
_____	_____
_____	_____
_____	_____
_____	_____
_____	_____
_____	_____
_____	_____
_____	_____

MAKING AN OUTLINE

This talk is a recipe. Before you outline the recipe, you can make a LIST of ingredients for REFERENCE. There are many steps in this recipe, so it's necessary to divide the steps into some STAGES.

Use the outline frame below. It has divided the steps into separate stages.

BANANA CAKE

INGREDIENTS: 1. lemon juice   6. salt
                 2. _____   7. _____
                 3. flour   8. _____
                 4. _____   9. walnuts
                 5. baking powder   10. _____

I.   Make the "sour milk."

    A.   Put _____ into

        a measuring cup

    B.   Add enough milk to make 2/3 of a cup.

    C.   Save this for later.

II. Prepare _____

    A.   _____ 3 or 4 _____

    B.   _____

III. Combine the dry ingredients

    A.   Put these items into a large bowl:

        1. _____ flour

        2. _____ sugar

        3. _____ salt

        4. _____ baking powder

    B.   _____

IV. Combine all the ingredients.

 A. Put the following things into the bowl (the same bowl that was used in Step III)

   1. _____

   2. _____ (from Step II)

   3. _____ (from Step I)

 B. _____ until everything gets wet.

 C. Add _____

 D. _____ 3-4 minutes.

 E. _____ walnuts.

V. Bake

 A. _____

   _____

 B. _____ 350 degrees Farenheit _____

 C. _____

APPLICATION

1. Use your completed outline to explain how to make "banana cake."

2. Look up a recipe (e.g. for bread, for a casserole dish, for a soup) in a cookbook or think of a recipe that you know. Make a brief outline of the steps. Explain how to do the recipe.

A GROUND BALL

■ VOCABULARY PREVIEW

The following words and expressions will appear in the talk. Listen and write a short definition for each item.

bounce— *to hit the hard surface and then go up into the air*

a bad bounce— *unusual unpredicable moment of the ball on the groud*

approach— *to move forward , to go forward*

base— *one of 4 position use in playing baseball*

baseball glove—*an item you wear on your hand when you play baseball that it use to catch the base ball*

■ SENTENCE CUES

Look at the following sentence patterns. Then listen to each sentence.

a.   As it *approach at you, stop moving* .

b.   It may be *difficult* to *catch* because *it come quickly* .

c.   *throw it* to the *base* where *the runner going* .

■ LISTENING STRATEGY

The speaker in this talk will explain a certain activity that you do when you play the game of baseball. The action is called "fielding a ground ball." As you listen, try to imagine what the action looks like.

Listen for verbs that indicate what the person should do: *approach, move, watch, reach, lower, be sure to…, etc.*

Now, listen to the talk.

Use this space (or additional paper) for your notes about the talk.

to fill the a grounder

☐ COMPREHENSION QUESTIONS

Listen to the questions and write your answers on the lines below.

1. _Why Should the fielder move approach the ball_
   to catch the ball

2. _Does ground ball always stay on the ground : No_
   _IS_ _The ground cane toast you and shirt bounce_

3. _Is the fielder suppose to pass to the ball_
   not he has to open the glove and ball bounce into it

4. _Should builder Stand up strayn while the fairly the ball : yes_
   Squta

5. _What then do with the ball after he catch it_

take it out of the throw builder
glove   toward the base where the runner going

AFTER YOU LISTEN

Tell the person directly what he's doing wrong. The correct actions are given in the talk.

You're not approaching the ball.
You're supposed to _____
_____.

You're not placing yourself in front of the ball.
You're supposed to _____
_____.

_____

_____

_____

_____

68

☐ COMPREHENSION QUESTIONS

Listen to the questions and write your answers on the lines below.

1. _Where did Classical music_ _____
   Europe hundred year ago

2. _Blue and enka are example What kind of music:_
   tradition

3. _What kind of instrument are use in rock music_
   Electrice instrument

4. _In which way jazz music is difference from another_
   rhythm _music_

5. _Give an example on kind of music that continentaly_
   classicand tradition Rock and Jazz

AFTER YOU LISTEN

Match the description with correct category. Use the information given in the talk.

R a. It originated in Europe.   JAZZ

R b. Electric instruments are often used.   ROCK

T c. "Enka" music is an example.   CLASSICAL

J d. It originated in Africa.   TRADITIONAL

T e. Each culture has its own kind.

R f. It has a strong beat.

R g. It began about 40 years ago.

C h. Bach and Beethoven composed this kind of music.

J i. It has a different rhythm from other kinds of music.

usic - Beethoven, Bach : Violin , Wind instrument

ago Europe , young people - 1960 - 1970 popular

71

MAKING AN OUTLINE

In your outline use the Roman numerals I, II, III, IV to indicate the MAIN HEADINGS. Use the capital letters A, B, C to indicate IMPORTANT FACTS. Use the Arabic numbers 1, 2, 3 to indicate EXAMPLES.

MUSIC

I. Classical music

    A.   Classical Music originated _____

    B.   Classical Music is played by _____

    _____

II. Traditional music

    A.   Traditional music comes from _____

        1. "Blues" comes from _____

        2. _____

    B.   Every culture has _____

    _____

III. _____

    A.   _____

    B.   _____

    C.   _____ instruments _____

IV. _____

    A.   _____

    B.   _____ special _____

    C.   _____ instruments can be used.

APPLICATION

1. Give a summary of this lesson's talk on music. Use your outline for reference.

2. Think of one kind of traditional music, a kind that you know well. Explain where the music came from, how old it is, what kind of instruments are used, etc. Make an outline before you begin your explanation.

ALFRED HITCHCOCK

■ VOCABULARY PREVIEW

The following words and expressions will appear in the talk. Listen and write a short definition for each item.

silent movie—

mystery—

novel—

script—

shoot a scene—

MOVIE TITLES: *The Pleasure Garden, Blackmail, Rebecca, Foreign Correspondent, Strangers on a Train, Suspicion, Family Plot, Psycho*

■ SENTENCE CUES

Look at the following sentence patterns. Then listen to each sentence.

a. *He used to _____ as _____ as he could.*

b. *He gave up the idea of _____ -ing _____ .*

c. *He did _____ by himself.*

■ LISTENING STRATEGY

This talk is about a famous film director named Alfred Hitchcock. You will be given some information about Hitchcock's career and some information about his background. The names of several movies are given in this talk.
Listen for the main events in his life and make note of some of his characteristics. Now, listen to the talk.

Use this space (or additional paper) for your notes about the talk.

□ COMPREHENSION QUESTIONS

Listen to the questions and write your answers on the lines below.

1. _____

2. _____

3. _____

4. _____

5. _____

AFTER YOU LISTEN

Match the phrase in Column A with an item in Column B.

Column A	Column B
1. his first movie	a. 1920
2. his birthplace	b. "Blackmail"
3. his first film company	c. London
4. his first talking movie	d. "The Pleasure Garden"
5. when he moved to California	e. California
6. when he was born	f. Islington Studios
7. his first movie in the U.S.	g. Hollywood
8. his last movie	h. 1899
9. the date of his last movie	i. 1980
	j. 1939
	k. "Rebecca"
	l. "Family Plot"
	m. 1976
	n. "Foreign Correspondent"
	o. The Famous Players

MAKING AN OUTLINE

We can divide Hitchcock's life into three parts: his early life, his professional life in England, and his professional life in the United States.

ALFRED HITCHCOCK

I. Early life

   A.   He was born _____

   B.   He studied _____

   C.   _____ interest _____

II. Professional life in England

   A.   His first job was _____

   B.   _____

       Islington Studios.

   C.   He directed his first _____

       ("The Pleasure Garden"—a silent movie)

   D.   He was known for _____

III. _____

   A.   _____ 1939.

   B.   He got most _____

       _____ (e.g. "Rebecca")

   C.   He chose all _____ and _____

       _____ by himself.

   D.   He made several more _____ in the U.S.

       1. Foreign Correspondent

       2. _____

       3. Psycho

       4. _____

APPLICATION

1. Give a summary of Alfred Hitchcock's life. Use your completed outline as a guide when you speak or write.

2. Think of another movie maker or writer. Find out about his/her life and work. Consult an encyclopedia or a biography of the person. Make an outline. Then give a short presentation.

LIFE EXPECTANCY

■ VOCABULARY PREVIEW

The following words and expressions will appear in the talk. Listen and write a short definition for each item.

expect/expectancy— *to predict of belive something happen*

century— *a previous of hundred year*

health care— *medical treatment taking care of your body*

developments— *advantage, new discovery*

■ SENTENCE CUES

Look at the following sentence patterns. Then listen to each sentence.

a.   Why does __it__ keep __get__-ing __high__-er and __high__-er?

b.   It varies from __country__ to __country__.

c.   It's a little __high__-er than __before__.

■ LISTENING STRATEGY

This talk will deal with the average life expectancy for humans. The speaker will give you some information about how the average life expectancy has changed in this century. You will hear several numbers and several specific years. Listen for these numbers and years.

Listen for these expressions that show that an explanation will follow: *actually, in fact, that means that....., so you can see that.....*

Now, listen to the talk.

Use this space (or additional paper) for your notes about the talk.

over 70 years
UAS   1980   73.8   higher than 1970 : 70.8

1900   - 47.3   1910 - 50   1920 : 59.1

1930   - 59.7   1940 62.9   1950 68.2

1960 : 69.7

26

health care improve
drug has been develop

☐ COMPREHENSION QUESTIONS

Listen to the questions and write your answers on the lines below.

1. Is the life expectancy average in every country?   No

2. In the U.SA how much the life expectancy increase has in the past 80 year 26.5

3. What was the life expectance average in the year 1900 47.30

4. What is one reason for the increase of expectancy: health care improve

5. What is another reason for the increase life expectancy drug has been developed

AFTER YOU LISTEN

Complete the following graph. The graph shows the increase in life expectancy in the United States from 1900 to 1980.

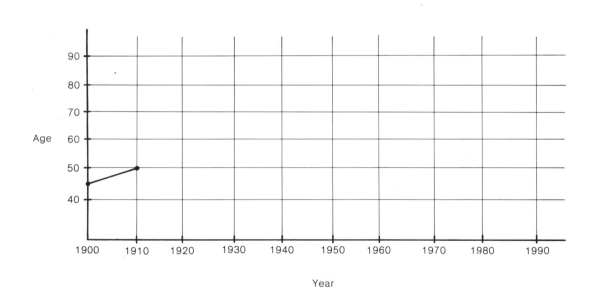

Year

MAKING AN OUTLINE

The first part of the talk is a LIST of numbers and dates. The second part attempts to EXPLAIN what the numbers mean or show.

LIFE EXPECTANCY

I. _____

    A.   1900 — 47.3

    B.   1910 — ____

    C.   1920 — 54.1

    D.   1930 — ____

    E.   1940 — 62.9

    F.   1950 — ____

    G.   ____ — ____

    H.   ____ — ____

    I.   ____ — ____

II. _____

    A. _____

        _____

    B. _____

APPLICATION

1.   Give a summary of this lesson's talk on "life expectancy." Use your finished outline for reference.

2.   Find out information about life expectancy for another country. Consult an almanac or other reference material. How has the life expectancy for that country changed? What are some reasons? Organize your information into an outline and prepare a graph. Then give a short presentation.

EARTHQUAKES

■ **VOCABULARY PREVIEW**

The following words and expressions will appear in the talk. Listen and write a short definition for each item.

the earth's crust— *the top layer of the earth*

plate— *round plat sheet of the material*

earthquake— *Violen shaken of the earth*

boundary— *the dividing point or dividing line between 2 area*

border— *divided line between 2 area*

curve— *to bend, to change the direction*

NAMES: Pacific, Atlantic, Indian Ocean, Antarctica, Eurasia, Australia, Africa, the Philippines, Indonesia, India, Thailand, Arabian Peninsula, Persian Gulf, Mediterranean Sea

■ **SENTENCE CUES**

Look at the following sentence patterns. Then listen to each sentence.

a. *Western* border is along *the coast of* *China*

b. All of *South of America* is contained on *this plate* .

c. *Earthquake* are most likely to happen at *these places*

■ **LISTENING STRATEGY**

This talk deals with how earthquakes occur. The speaker will describe different "plates" of the "crust" of the earth. Listen for the general boundaries of the plates and also listen for the cause of earthquakes.

Listen for expressions of location like these: *through the middle of the Atlantic Ocean, continues to the east to Iran, along southern Asia, extends to the west coast of North America, curves back to the south.*

Now, listen to the talk.

Use this space (or additional paper) for your notes about the talk.

1) North American
2) South American
3) Pacific place

79

☐ COMPREHENSION QUESTIONS

Listen to the questions and write your answers on the lines below.

1. What is the top layer of the earth call? Earth's Cru

2. the earth crust divided into how many major session
   7

3. What causes the earthquakes: 2 plate push against each
   most other or 2 plate

4. Which the 3 country likely to have Earth quake
   Brazil (Japan), Australia

5. Which is the largest of the earth major plate
   pacific.

AFTER YOU LISTEN

Below is a map of the world, divided according to the boundaries of the major plates of the earth's crust. Each plate has a number. Give the name of each plate; match with the numbers on the map.

1. _____   5. _____

2. _____   6. _____

3. _____   7. _____

4. _____

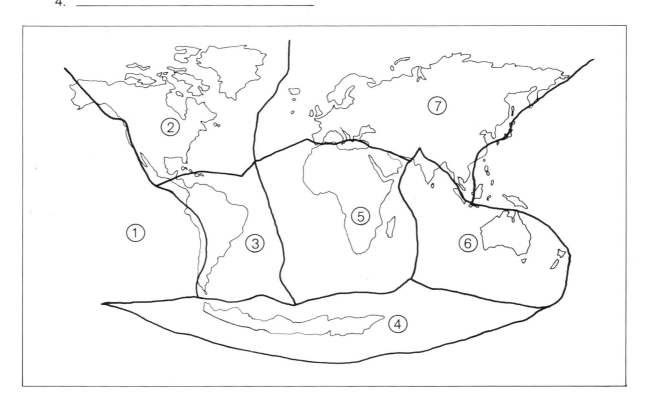

80

MAKING AN OUTLINE

This talk explains the CAUSE of earthquakes and then describes the boundaries of the plates. Your outline will probably be divided into two parts as such.

EARTHQUAKES

I. Cause

    A. _____ is divided into plates

    B. _____

       _____

II. The major plates (for exact boundaries, see map)

    A. _____ Plate—west coast of N.A., middle of Atlantic

       Ocean, central Mexico.

    B. _____ Plate—middle of Mexico, middle of Atlantic

       Ocean, west coast of South America.

    C. _____ Plate—S.A. and N.A. plate on east, Japan, east

       coast of China, to Indonesia.

    D. _____ Plate—west coast of southeast Asia, up to north-

       ern India, Indian Ocean.

    E. _____ Plate—Persian Gulf, Mediterranean Sea, N.A. and

       S.A. Plates.

    F. _____ Plate—N.A. Plate, African Plate, Australian Plate,

       N.A. Plate.

    G. _____ Plate—Pacific Plate, Australian Plate, S.A. Plate.

APPLICATION

1.   Use your outline and a map to summarize this lesson s talk on earthquakes.

2.   Earthquakes are a natural phenomenon: they occur according to natural laws. Think of another natural phenomenon (e.g. thunder storms, tornados, volcanos' erupting). Consult reference books to find out why and how they occur. Put your information into an outline. Then give a short presentation. Your presentation can be written or spoken.

MAKING PEARLS

▫ VOCABULARY PREVIEW

The following words and expressions will appear in the talk. Listen and write a short definition for each item.

oyster—

irritate—

get rid of—

protect—

insert—

■ SENTENCE CUES

Look at the following sentence patterns. Then listen to each sentence.

a.   *It _____ by _____ -ing _____ .*

b.   *_____ instead of _____ -ing _____ .*

c.   *_____ not _____ enough to _____ .*

■ LISTENING STRATEGY

> This talk deals with how pearls are made, both naturally and by manufacturers. The manufacturing process is actually quite similar to the natural process. Listen for how pearls are formed.
> Now, listen to the talk.

Use this space (or additional paper) for your notes about the talk.

☐ COMPREHENSION QUESTIONS

Listen to the questions and write your answers on the lines below.

1. _____

2. _____

3. _____

4. _____

5. _____

AFTER YOU LISTEN

1) Fill in the blanks in the following paragraph.

If a _____ of sand enters the _____ shell,

it will try to _____ the sand. If it is

unable to _____ , it will _____

the sand with a _____ . This _____

will later _____ a pearl. It _____

seven years for a _____ to _____

2) Match the word on the left with its correct definition on the right.

irritate   a. to throw out, to eliminate

get rid of   b. to surround, to enclose

protect   c. to place inside of something

cover   d. to bother, to hurt, to upset

insert   e. to guard, to keep from danger or pain

MAKING AN OUTLINE

This talk describes two types of pearls and how they are "produced." Your outline will have to give both processes separately.

MAKING PEARLS

I. Pearls are made by _____

   A. Sand _____

      1. The sand _____

      2. The oyster _____

   B. The oyster _____

      1. If the oyster can't _____ it _____

         _____

      2. _____

   C. The liquid _____

      1. It takes about _____

      2. Only a few _____

II. Pearls are "manufactured" by people.

   A. _____

   B. _____

   C. _____

   D. _____

   E. _____ it after 7 years.

   F. _____

      1. _____

      2. _____

APPLICATION

1. Summarize this lesson's talk. Use your complete outline for reference.

2. Pearls are formed by a biological process. Think of a biological process that takes place in humans (e.g. digestion, breathing, sleeping). Explain how it occurs. Before you give your presentation, look up the necessary information, take notes, and organize your notes into an outline.

DIZZY GILLESPIE

■ VOCABULARY PREVIEW

The following words and expressions will appear in the talk. Listen and write a short definition for each item.

amateur— *not professional*

trumpet— *a wind instrument*

trombone— *another wind instrument*

recording session— *any vanes at recording studio in which musician play music that will record all the records*

bandleader— *the person who conduct or leeded musician*

personality— *a person character or characteristics other What the person is like*

NAMES: Lionel Hampton, Charlie Parker, Ella Fitzgerald, Freddie Hubbard, Blue Mitchell

■ SENTENCE CUES

Look at the following sentence patterns. Then listen to each sentence.

a. *Whenever* _he had a change, he use to play the instrument_.

b. *By the time* _he was 13_, _he has be complex good!_

c. *Other* _musician_-s who have _work_ -ed _repect him_ .

■ LISTENING STRATEGY

This is a talk about a famous musician named Dizzy Gillespie. You will hear some information about Gillespie's background and about his career.
Listen for a description of some of the main events in his life. Also take note of some of his personal characteristics.
Now, listen to the talk.

Use this space (or additional paper) for your notes about the talk.

Jazz King of trumpet , 1917 ; South Carolina
John Bus Gillespie ; unusual ; crazzy
1936 Philadephia - musician ; 1937 play and recordiy session

1996 : Start his own band , 25 year travely
Afria Europe , American

□ COMPREHENSION QUESTIONS

Listen to the questions and write your answers on the lines below.

1. What does the nick nain dizzy mean? Unusual, crazzy

2. Who are Lionel Hampton and Charlie Parker? Famous

3. Why did Gillepie accept young men in his band? he went to teach and learn new type

4. What kind of instrument Gillepie like to play? trumpet, trumbone Wind instrument

5. Did Gillepie studied music in the college music school? No

AFTER YOU LISTEN

Write an event in Gillespie's life for each date.

1917 — _____

1930 — _____

1936 — _____

1937 — _____

1946 — _____

MAKING AN OUTLINE

This talk was a short biography. Sometimes it is useful to divide a biography into periods in the person's life. In this case we can divide Gillespie's life into perhaps two periods: his early life and his musical career.

DIZZY GILLESPIE

I. _____

   A.   He grew up in _____

   B.   He learned to _____

   C.   _____ "Dizzy."

   D.   _____ scholarship _____

II. _____

   A.   He had several important experiences early in his career.

      1. His first job was _____

      _____

      2. _____ in 1937.

      3. He worked with many _____

   B.   _____

      1. _____ travelling _____

      _____

      2. His band members find him _____

      _____

APPLICATION

1. Give a summary of this talk on Dizzy Gillespie. Use your outline for reference.

2. Think of a well known musician (or other artist) from any country. Prepare to give a short presentation on this person. Organize your information into an outline first.

ASSASSINATION THEORIES

■ VOCABULARY PREVIEW

The following words and expressions will appear in the talk. Listen and write a short definition for each item.

theory—

assassination—

trial—

shoot—

insist—

conspiracy—

participate—

complicated—

■ SENTENCE CUES

The following sentences (or similar sentences) will appear in the talk.

a. *According to* _____ , _____ .

b. *In spite of* _____ , _____ .

c. *They think that* _____ *must have* _____ *-ed* _____ .

■ LISTENING STRATEGY

In 1963 the President of the United States, John Kennedy, was killed. This talk deals with the assassination of Kennedy. The speaker will briefly explain two theories about who killed Kennedy. Listen for the differences between the two theories.
Now, listen to the talk.

Use this space (or additional paper) for your notes about the talk.

☐ COMPREHENSION QUESTIONS

Listen to the questions and write your answers on the lines below.

1. _____

2. _____

3. _____

4. _____

5. _____

AFTER YOU LISTEN

Fill in the table. For each space, write YES, NO, or PERHAPS.

Question	according to the Single Assassin Theory	according to the Conspiracy Theory
a. Did one person plan Kennedy's assassination?		
b. Did Oswald shoot Kennedy?		
c. Did Ruby know Oswald?		
d. Was Oswald a member of a group that planned to kill Kennedy?		
e. Could one person only have planned the assassination?		

MAKING AN OUTLINE

When you make an outline, you can divide the talk into explanations of TWO THEORIES (I, II). Capital letters (A, B, C) will give KEY FACTS about those theories.

ASSASSINATION THEORIES

I. The Single-Assassin Theory

    A.   Lee Harvey Oswald acted _____

    B.   Jack Ruby, the man who _____ , was not _____

    C.   Oswald denied _____

    D.   _____ believe this theory _____

II. The Conspiracy Theory

    A.   _____ planned Kennedy's _____

    B.   Oswald might have been a _____

    C.   Ruby might have been a _____

    D.   Perhaps the conspiracy wanted Oswald to _____

         _____

    E.   People who believe this theory think that Kennedy's assassination was _____

         _____

         _____

APPLICATION

LANGUAGE FAMILIES

■ VOCABULARY PREVIEW

The following words and expressions will appear in the talk. Listen and write a short definition for each item.

local language— *in the language spoken in a smal area of an oranation country*

dialects— *form of language that it use in one area with some one differrent*

NAMES: Indo-European, Afro-Asiatic, Bantu, Sino-Tibetan, Polynesian, Arabic, Chinese, English, French, Greek, Hausa, Swahili, Thai, Vietnamese, Zulu

from other form of language

■ SENTENCE CUES

Look at the following sentence patterns. Then listen to each sentence.

a. *Almost all of these* __languages__ *-s* __belong to a small number of family__

b. *Even though there are* __a lot of languages__ *, there aren't* __so many language family__

c. __Languages__ *such as* __French and Greek belong to this family__ .

■ LISTENING STRATEGY

This talk will describe some large families of languages. As you listen take note of the different families that are described. Listen for the general location where the languages of each family are spoken. A large number of language names and place names will be used in this talk.
Now, listen to the talk.

＊ Polynesian: island language : Indonesia East world all the way to Hawaii Island west off the way to Alaska : Hawaiian

Use this space (or additional paper) for your notes about the talk.

3,000 language

Similar: Sound, grammar, the way they think, talk

20 - 30 major language family

＊ English : Indo-European, French, Spanish

＊ Afro Asiatic : Middle East, Nort Africa : Arabic, Hausa

＊ bantu : Central and Southern Africa : Swahili, Zulu

＊ Sino-Tibetan: Chinese 800,000,000 , South-East Asia : Vietnamese, Th... 250,000;

☐ COMPREHENSION QUESTIONS

Listen to the questions and write your answers on the lines below.

1. In what way are the language within the same ~~language family~~ similar?
   3 point : Gramar , Vocabulary, Sound
2. About how many major language family are there?
   20-30 major language
3. The languages are spoken in the middle East are member with which language family? Afro Asiatic
4. Are all the language spoken in East-Asia member of Sino-Tibetan family? no like Japaness
5. How did the polynesian language probaly spread?
   traveler island to island and each group islash develope it own invidial language

AFTER YOU LISTEN

Look at the map below. Which language families do the numbers indicate?

1. _____   4. _____

2. _____   5. _____

3. _____

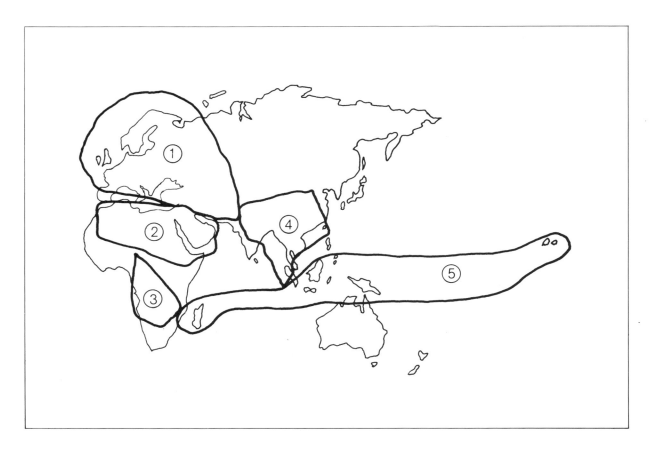

MAKING AN OUTLINE

This talk gives a definition of "language families" (I) and then describes some large language families (II).

LANGUAGE FAMILIES

I. Language Families—Definition

    A. _____

    B. _____ are similar.

    C. _____ is similar.

II. Some Large Language Families

    A. Indo-European

       1. Indo-European languages are spoken throughout Europe.

       2. Some languages in this family are _____

       _____

    B. Afro-Asiatic _____

       1. _____

       _____

       2. _____

       _____

    C. Bantu

       1. Bantu languages are spoken in _____

       _____

       2. _____

       _____

    D. _____

       1. _____

       _____ Asia.

       2. _____

       _____

E. _____

    1. _____

      _____

    2. _____

      _____

APPLICATION

1. Use your outline and a map to summarize this lesson's talk on language families.

2. Select one area of the world (e.g. the Middle East, Eastern Europe, Southeast Asia). Find out what languages are spoken in that area. Make a list of your information. Then give a short presentation.

MARGARET MEAD

■ VOCABULARY PREVIEW

The following words and expressions will appear in the talk. Listen and write a short definition for each item.

social science—

contribution—

anthropology—

primitive society—

fieldwork—

emphasize—

interfere—

■ SENTENCE CUES

Look at the following sentence patterns. Then listen to each sentence.

a. _____ *are rather different from* _____ .

b. *If he wants to* _____ , *then he can't* _____ .

c. *It's a study of* _____ , *particularly* _____ .

■ LISTENING STRATEGY

The speaker in this talk will speak about Margaret Mead, a famous anthropologist. Two areas will be discussed: Mead's fieldwork and Mead's methods. As you listen, take note of Mead's work in these areas.
Now, listen to the talk.

Use this space (or additional paper) for your notes about the talk.

□ COMPREHENSION QUESTIONS

Listen to the questions and write your answers on the lines below.

1. _____

2. _____

3. _____

4. _____

5. _____

AFTER YOU LISTEN

1) Fill in the table with information from the talk.

Mead's Field Work

Place	Dates

2) Read the passage below, which was written by Margaret Mead. Then answer (true or false) the questions which follow.

...When the anthropologist enters the village of a primitive people... the situation is a controlled and conscious one. He does not want to understand the culture *so that* he can get a house built, a garden dug, carriers for his gear, labourers on a new air-field, or converts for his religion. He does not even, as a doctor would, want to cure them of their diseases or change their ideas about public health... He does not want to improve them, convert them, govern them, trade with them, recruit them, or heal them. He wants only to understand them, and by understanding them to add to our knowledge of the limitations and potentialities of human beings.

Margaret Mead, from *Male and Female,* 1950.

1. The anthropologist should try to understand the culture in order to find people who can help him. (True/False)

2. The anthropologist should act like a doctor and try to improve the health of the people. (True/False)

3. The anthropologist wants to add to our knowledge of human beings. (True/False)

MAKING AN OUTLINE

This talk is a kind of biography, but it focusses on two major TOPICS or THEMES. Your outline will also focus on these two topics (i.e. Mead's two major contributions to social science).

MARGARET MEAD (1901-78);

Three Major Contributions to Social Science

I. Research of primitive societies

    A.   Definition of "primitive society"

        1. _____

        2. _____

        3. _____

    B.   Mead's first field work.

        1. 1925-26 in _____

        2. Observations are recorded in *Coming of Age in Samoa* (1928).

        3. Her studies dealt with _____

           _____

    C.   Other field work

        1. _____ (1928-29)

        2. _____ (1931-33)

        3. _____ (1936-38)

    D.   Results of her studies

        1. Knowledge about _____

        2. _____

        3. _____

II. _____

   A. _____

      1. _____

      2. _____

      3. _____

   B. _____

      1. The anthropologist should not want to _____

_____

      2. Other interests interfere with _____

APPLICATION

1. Give a brief summary of this lesson's talk on Margaret Mead.

2. Think of another person who has worked in the area of anthropology, sociology, politics, or education. Find out about his/her life and work. Consult an encyclopedia or a biography of the person. Make an outline of your information. Then give a short presentation.

APPENDIX

Vocabulary for Review

APPENDIX

Vocabulary for Review

An asterisk (*) indicates that the word listed is beyond the 3000 word frequency range, as approximated by the New Horizon Ladder Dictionary of the English Language (Signet: New York, 1970).

	Verbs	Nouns	Adjectives
T-1			
	require	team	separate
	compete	individual	competitive
	play	competition	main
	win	exercise	possible
	perform	difference	individual
			alone
T-2			
	crack	omelette	both
	add	bowl	other
	cut	chopsticks	same
	mix	mixture	
	light	ingredients	
	melt	piece	
	stick		
	pour		
	cook		
	remove		
T-3			
	block	village	impossible
	move	earthquake	amazed
	push	rope	
	roll	course	
	shout	shovel	
	laugh	dirt	
	uncover	sphere	
	bury	incline	
	smile		
	destroy		
	dig		
T-4			
	spread	muscle	straight
	lie	chest	normal
	straighten	shoulder	face-down
	lower	floor	immediate
	touch	weight	
	rise		
	support		

	Verbs	Nouns	Adjectives
T-5	divide	calendar	ancient
	repeat	significance*	suitable
	suit	choice	
	select	partner	
	consult	marriage	
	keep track of	profession	
		meaning	
		chart*	
T-6	lift	hips	heavy
	squat	knees	straight
	bend	object	direct
	hurt	waist	
	pick up		
	remember		
T-7	explain	cylinder*	narrow
	extend	combination	correct
	fit	metal	flat
	require	disc*	special
	turn	dial	
		instrument	
		knowledge	
T-8	install*	wire	straight
	pass	problem	confused
	solve	pipe	
	carry	mouse	
	tie	male	
	untie	female	
	hold		
	squeeze		
	understand		
T-9	list	spelling	obvious
	pronounce	pronounciation	particular
	look up	alphabet	alphabetical
	depend		approximate
			common
			different
			important

	Verbs	**Nouns**	**Adjectives**
T-10	double	trick	final
	add	step	first
	multiply	address	last
	subtract	example	
		result	
		total	
T-11	protect	substance	natural
	contain	skin	healthy
	stay	source	necessary
		variety	essential
		grain	various
		nerve	sufficient
		health	
		brain	
		bone	
		kidney*	
		oxygen	
T-12	determine	difficulty	rough
	define	suburb	metropolitan*
	compare	estimate	
	increase	limit	
	mention	boundary	
	surround	population	
	estimate	resident	
T-13	refer	statistics*	middle
	calculate	quantity	expected
	eliminate	score	average
		order	misleading
		average	unusual
		arithmetic	typical
			realistic
T-14	follow	shell	basic
	grow	tray	entire
	roast	paste	
	improve	spice	
	crush	flavor	
	grind*	tub	
	transport		
	pick		

	Verbs	Nouns	Adjectives
T-15			
	connect	device	important
	produce	electricity	quick
	contain	groove*	
	escape		
	burn out		
	conduct		
T-16			
	attack	boar	favorite
	catch	trap	gentle
	get rid of	cage	wild
	accept	weapon	
	arrive	behavior	
	cause	diary	
	worry	conclusion	
	prefer	section	
	believe	fence	
	continue	gate	
	spread	material	
	feed		
	bother		
T-17			
	concern	expression	minor
	spell	vowel	exact
		dialect*	different
		compartment*	
		idiom*	
T-18			
	describe	answer	single
	perform	digit*	
	consist	magic	
	choose	series	
	omit	factor	
	repeat		
T-19			
	dry	process	oval-shaped
	cool	taste	ripe
	boil	row	bitter
			tropical
			rich
			sweet

	Verbs	Nouns	Adjectives
T-20	measure stir crush mash beat chop remove continue	teaspoon degree measuring cup oven	sour wet thorough moist
T-21	throw bounce approach face reach take out place	ground hop finger glove runner base	shy strange quick direct
T-22	originate refer compose	category culture instrument composer	musical traditional popular original
T-23	give up direct create complete select decide	mystery script novel assistant	famous strict clever complex
T-24	expect cure develop vary rise improve prevent	disease century expectancy reason information	related powerful fatal steady

	Verbs	**Nouns**	**Adjectives**
T-25	compose	crust	eastern
	rub	section	western
	shake	motion	northern
	curve	coast	southern
	extend	border	
	cover	boundary	
	touch	layer	
	surround	plate	
	occur		
T-26	irritate	gem	valuable
	injure	oyster*	rough
	form	fluid	smooth
	swallow		
	spit		
	discover		
	insert*		
	attempt		
	manufacture		
T-27	experiment	influence	actual
	recognize	amateur*	crazy
	travel	lung	comfortable
	prefer	scholarship*	patient
	record	personality	fair
	accept	style	modern
		career	
T-28	kill	theory	responsible
	insist	trial	single
	participate	member	involved
	discuss	conspiracy*	complicated
	plan	murder	
	shoot		
	assassinate*		
	believe		
	conclude		
T-29	include	island	similar
	belong	member	major
	spread	grammar	unrelated
	develop	style	
		history	

Verbs	Nouns	Adjectives

T-30

Verbs	Nouns	Adjectives
die	contribution	interested
record	customs	primitive
publish	facility	accurate
locate	goal	
raise	scientist	
gather	role	
emphasize	custom	
trade	research	
observe	adolescence	
interfere		